WEIRD WEATHER

CREEPY CLOUDS

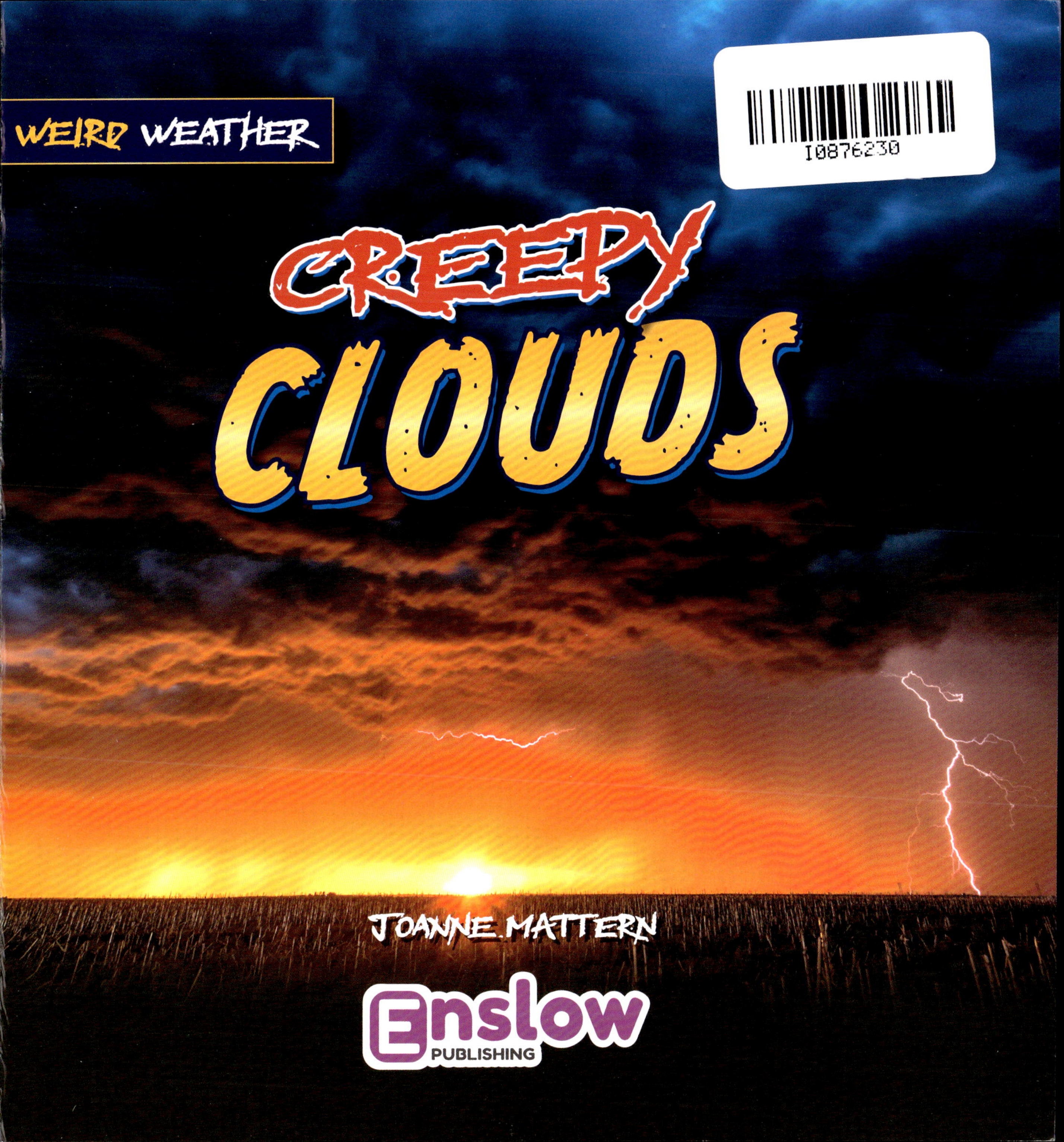

JOANNE MATTERN

Enslow PUBLISHING

Please visit our website, www.enslow.com. For a free color catalog of all our high-quality books, call toll free 1-800-398-2504 or fax 1-877-980-4454

Published in 2027 by
Enslow Publishing
2544 Clinton Street
Buffalo, NY 14224

Cataloging-in-Publication Data
Names: Mattern, Joanne, 1963-.
Title: Creepy clouds / Joanne Mattern.
Description: Buffalo, NY : Enslow Publishing, 2027. | Series: Weird weather | Includes glossary.
Identifiers: ISBN 9781978549692 (pbk.) | ISBN 9781978549708 (library bound) | ISBN 9781978549715 (ebook)
Subjects: LCSH: Clouds--Juvenile literature. | Atmosphere--Juvenile literature. | Sky--Juvenile literature. | Weather--Juvenile literature.
Classification: LCC QC921.35 M375 2027 | DDC 551.576--dc23

Photos Credits: Cover, p.1 ©2020 Joe Belanger/Shutterstock.com; p.3 and throughout the book ©2020 Cherisha Kay Norman/Shutterstock.com; p.4 ©2019 Suzanne Tucker, ©2020 Dudarev Mikhail/Shutterstock.com; p.5 ©2024 BEST-BACKGROUNDS/Shutterstock.com; p.6 ©2021 Mny-Jhee/Shutterstock.com; p.6, p.7 ©2022 Suzanne Tucker/Shutterstock.com; p.8 ©2021 ANTIVAR/Shutterstock.com; p.9 ©2021 BlueRingMedia/Shutterstock.com; p.10 ©2012 Vasik Olga/Shutterstock.com; p.11, p.28 ©2014 Semmick Photo/Shutterstock.com; p.12 ©2022 Sara Wiza/Shutterstock.com; p.13, p.29 ©2018 Menno van der Haven/Shutterstock.com; p.14 ©2022 Silverszay/Shutterstock.com; p.15 ©2016 VarnakovR/Shutterstock.com; p.16, p.29 ©2019 pr2is/Shutterstock.com; p.17 ©2018 Menno van der Haven/Shutterstock.com; p.18 ©2017 aapsky/Shutterstock.com; p.19 ©2021 kevinm1013/Shutterstock.com; p.20, p.21 ©2018 Red Buffalo Studios/Shutterstock.com; p.22 ©2019 Chaleephoto/Shutterstock.com; p.23, p.28 ©2025 Romija/Shutterstock.com; p.24 ©2021 Bronmik/Shutterstock.com; p.25, p.29 ©2013 Christian Mueller/Shutterstock.com; p.26, p.27 ©2024 Strikernia/Shutterstock.com

Printed in China

CPSIA compliance information: Batch #QSENS27: For further information, contact Enslow Publishing, New York, New York, at 1-800-398-2504.

TABLE OF CONTENTS

Words in the glossary appear in **bold** type the first time they are used in the text.

CLOUD SURFING!

You've probably heard of people surfing on ocean waves. But what about surfing on clouds? There is a special place in Australia where unusual clouds make surfing possible.

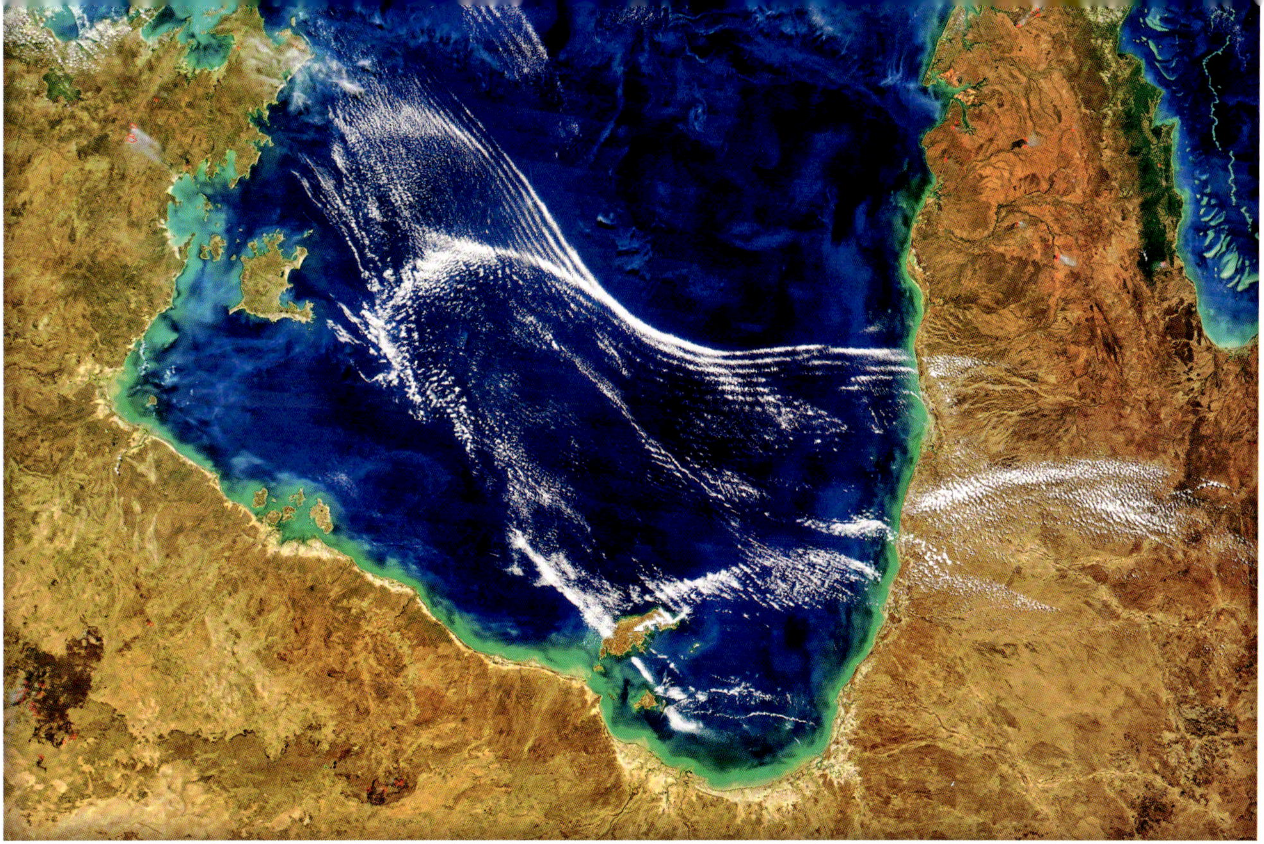

Welcome to the Gulf of Carpentaria. For part of the year, the land is dry. Then, in October or November, wet weather moves in. Hot air and cold **air masses** collide. The result is something called Morning Glory clouds.

Morning Glory clouds look like long rolls or tubes. The wind moves them so fast, the waves can be measured on graphs that show earthquakes. It's creepy to think wind and clouds can be that strong!

During the 1980s, some people tried hang-gliding on the Morning Glory. It was fun! Soon, other people decided to try it too. Today, many people go to the Gulf to cloud surf. They let the rushing wind move them through the roll clouds. It's like ocean waves moving a surfer through the water.

Roll clouds are just one of the strange types of clouds on planet Earth. Let's discover more of these amazing—and sometimes creepy—clouds!

MOVEMENT OF THE GODS

Australia's indigenous people believe Walalu, the Rainbow Serpent, creates the Morning Glory to watch over the people.

WHAT ARE CLOUDS?

Clouds may look solid, but they're not. Some clouds are made of tiny water droplets. Others are made of ice crystals. That water and ice can turn clouds into some creepy forms!

Clouds form when water **vapor condenses** in the sky. These droplets condense around bits of dust or salt in the air.

Clouds don't all look the same. Cirrus clouds are thin and wispy. Cumulus clouds are tall and fluffy. Stratus clouds form in sheets. They can cover the whole sky like a blanket.

One scary kind of cloud is called a cumulonimbus cloud. These clouds are big and tall. Sometimes they are gray or black. They contain a lot of **moisture**. You'll often see cumulonimbus clouds during a thunderstorm or a tornado. Creepy weather alert!

SKY SAUCERS

Is that a flying saucer in the sky? No! That strange, saucer-shaped form is a lenticular cloud.

Lenticular clouds often form over mountains. That's because the mountain gets in the way of the wind. When air flows over a mountain, it creates waves on one side. If there is a lot of moisture in the air, the water vapor will condense into a cloud. The waves of air stretch the cloud into a saucer shape as the wind moves down the mountain.

Lenticular clouds are pretty. But airplane pilots avoid them. That's because the moving wind can cause a lot of **turbulence**.

UNIDENTIFIED FLYING OBJECTS

Some reports of UFO sightings turned out to be lenticular clouds.

CLOUD POUCHES

Cumulus clouds usually build upward. They are tall. But sometimes the moisture in a cloud hangs downward. This creates a mammatus cloud.

Mammatus clouds often form at the bottom of a cumulonimbus cloud. Instead of moving up, turbulence in the clouds pushes the cold air and ice crystals down. These droplets hang in pouches at the bottom of the cloud. Each pouch can be up to 1.9 miles (three kilometers) in diameter.

If you see a mammatus cloud, you'd best get inside. These clouds can signal violent weather is on the way.

A STORM IS COMING

Anvil clouds are another sign of thunderstorms. These creepy clouds are flat on top, like an anvil.

WAVES IN THE SKY

When warm and cold air meet, interesting things happen! Often, these meetings are violent. Thunderstorms and tornadoes both occur when warm and cold air hit each other. But not all of these meetings are bad.

Asperitas clouds are rare. They need **unstable** conditions to form. Sometimes you might see them before or after a thunderstorm. But they often occur during calm weather as well.

This cloud got its name from the Latin word *aspero*. *Aspero* means "rough." These creepy clouds look rough and uneven.

WELCOME TO THE CLUB!

Asperitas clouds were added to the International Cloud Atlas in 2015. They are the newest cloud to be added.

FALLING SKIES

Have you ever seen a big hole in the middle of the clouds? This is called a fallstreak hole. A fallstreak hole is caused by really cold air.

The water droplets in a cumulus cloud are very cold. But they aren't quite frozen. If something introduces colder air, the droplets will freeze, become heavier, and fall. As they drop down, they leave a hole in the clouds. The hole will get bigger as surrounding droplets freeze too.

What can introduce super-cold air? Airplanes! When a plane passes through a cloud, air moves over its wings. This air cools as it travels over the plane. If conditions are just right, a fallstreak hole will form.

HOLE PUNCH CLOUDS

Fallstreak holes are also called hole punch clouds. You can probably figure out why!

Rare and Beautiful

One of the most beautiful cloud formations has the longest name. Kelvin-Helmholtz clouds are hardly ever seen. But if you get the chance, you will likely never forget the sight!

Kelvin-Helmholtz are a type of cirrus clouds. Cirrus clouds are very common. These thin clouds often appear high in the sky during good weather. But Kelvin-Helmholtz clouds are different.

These clouds might appear on windy days. Wind can blow in different layers. Sometimes the top layer blows faster than the layer below it. When this happens, the air movement makes the tops of the clouds form into the shape of ocean waves.

Kelvin-Helmholtz clouds are named after two scientists. The first is a British scientist called Baron Kelvin. The second is a German scientist named Hermann von Helmholtz. Both men studied unstable wind patterns in the air.

Kelvin-Helmholtz clouds look pretty. But they can be dangerous! Because the wind is unstable, it can create turbulence. This can be a big problem for airplanes.

These special clouds are not just found on Earth. Scientists have spotted them on Jupiter and Saturn too. They have even been seen on the surface of the Sun!

COLORFUL CLOUDS

Some of the most colorful clouds form at the North and South Poles. Why? The air at these places is very cold. These clouds are called nacreous clouds, or polar stratospheric clouds. The **stratosphere** is one of the layers of Earth's atmosphere.

Nacreous clouds are known for their bright colors. These colors form when sunlight hits the ice crystals in the clouds. The crystals break the light into different colors. It's like the rainbows that form when light shines through a prism.

BRRR!

Nacreous clouds can only form when the temperature is –121 degrees Fahrenheit (–85 degrees Celsius) or colder.

Fog and Smog

Walking through fog is like walking through a cloud. That's because fog is a cloud! It's just closer to the ground. If **visible** water vapor is more than 50 feet (15 meters) above the ground, it is a cloud. Any lower and it is called fog.

Fog can be pretty. It makes everything look strange. Familiar shapes look different than they did before. But fog can also be creepy. It is hard to see in fog. Driving and boating are dangerous in foggy weather.

FOG FORMATION

Fog often forms over bodies of water. This happens when warm air flows over cooler water.

Fog can be dangerous. But smog can be even worse. Smog is a combination of two words: *smoke* and *fog*. Smog can make the air hazy and hard to see through, just like fog. But smog is more dangerous because of what it holds.

Smog is filled with air pollution. It has smoke and harmful chemicals in it. Smog also contains a gas called ozone. Ozone can make it very hard to breathe.

Clouds come in many different shapes and types. Some are beautiful. Some are dangerous. Next time you are outside, look up at the sky. You never know what clouds might be drifting over your head!

DEADLY AIR

In 1952, thick smog covered London for five days. Thousands of people died.

WHAT AM I?

Can you guess what type of creepy cloud is shown in each photo? Look closely at these images and use the clues to help you figure it out. Then, check your answers below. How many did you get right?

1

I might look like a UFO, but I'm not. I form when air flows over mountains and creates waves. What am I?

2

I am full of bright colors like a sunset. But it's ice crystals that make me glow. What am I?

3

It's easy to get lost when I come down to Earth. What am I?

4

A circle is my favorite shape! I form when water droplets fall through the middle of me. What am I?

5

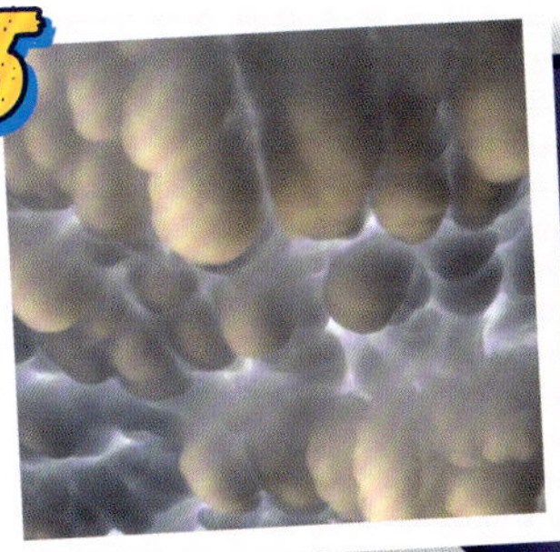

Things can get rough when my pouch-like clouds form. What am I?

1. lenticular cloud; 2. nacreous cloud; 3. fog; 4. fallstreak hole; 5. mammatus cloud

GLOSSARY

air masses (air mas-siz): groupings of air in the atmosphere that have about the same temperature and amount of moisture

condenses (kun-DEN-sez): changes from a gas to a liquid

moisture (MOYS-chur): dampness

stratosphere (STRAT-uh-sfeer): the layer of Earth's atmosphere that begins about eight miles (12.9 kilometers) above Earth and ends about 31 miles (50 kilometers) above Earth

turbulence (TUR-byuh-lenss): violent movement of air or water

unstable (uhn-STAY-buhl): not steady; likely to change

vapor (VAY-pur): a gas formed from something that is usually a liquid or solid at normal temperatures

visible (VIZ-uh-buhl): able to be seen

FACT CHECK

1. Lenticular clouds form when mountains block the ___________.
   a. wind b. rain c. snow
2. Cirrus clouds form when the weather is ___________.
   a. cold b. stormy c. clear
3. Fog is dangerous because it makes it hard to ___________.
   a. breathe b. see c. stay warm

Answers: 1. a, 2. c, 3. b

FURTHER READING

Gleisner, Jenna Lee. *Clouds.* Jump! Inc., 2025.
Perdew, Laura. *Natural Wonders.* The Child's World, 2025.
Rossiter, Brienna. *Fog.* North Star Editions, 2019.

ON THE INTERNET

Cloud
https://kids.britannica.com/students/article/cloud/273708
This Britannica Kids article explains how clouds form and describes the different types.

Types of Clouds: Discover the 4 Main Cloud Groups
https://a-z-animals.com/blog/types-of-clouds-discover-the-4-main-cloud-groups/
Check out descriptions, charts, and photos of the many different types of clouds.

Publisher's note to educators and parents: Our editors have carefully reviewed these websites to ensure that they are suitable for students. Many websites change frequently, however, and we cannot guarantee that a site's future contents will continue to meet our high standards of quality and educational value. Be advised that students should be closely supervised whenever they access the internet.

INDEX

ABOUT THE AUTHOR

Joanne Mattern is the author of many books for children on a variety of subjects, including science, history, and biography. She loves writing about and experiencing weird weather events! Joanne loves to learn about people, places, and events and bring historical figures to life for today's readers. She lives in New York State with her family.